Bounty

BOUNTY

Landeg White

Dangaroo Press

4

Plates:
'Heads of divers Natives of the Islands of Otaheite, Huaheine & Oheiteroah'. Plate VIII from *A Journal of a Voyage to the South Seas in his Majesty's Ship* Endeavour. © The Natural History Museum, London. Reproduced by permission.

'Hibiscus Rosa Sinensis' and 'Uru Artocarpus altilis'. Paintings by Sydney Parkinson (1769). Photo refs. T01921/R and T01917/A. © The Natural History Museum, London. Reproduced by permission.

Extracts from the song 'She wears red feathers' reproduced by permission of Warner Chappell Music Ltd/International Music Publications.

Yorkshire & Humberside
A R T S

© Landeg White, 1993

ISBN 1 - 871049 03 2   7|12|93

Published by Dangaroo Press
Australia: G.P.O. Box 1209, Sydney, New South Wales, 2001
Denmark: Geding Søvej 21, 8381 Mundelstrup
UK: P.O. Box 20, Hebden Bridge, West Yorkshire HX7 5UZ

Design and layout by Glenda Pattenden and Tim Caudery

Printed in Great Britain by Villiers Publications, London N3

for

Martin Kondwane

wishing him bounty

Acknowledgements

My principal sources have been O. Rutter (ed), *The Trial of the 'Bounty' Mutineers* (Edinburgh, 1931), Douglas L. Oliver, *Ancient Tahitian Society* 3 Vol. (University of Hawaii Press, 1974), and Lt. Wm Bligh, *The Log of HMS Bounty 1787-89* (Guildford: Genesis Publications, 1975).

The opening and closing sections are adapted from Hugh Carrington (ed), *The Discovery of Tahiti: A Journal of the second voyage of HMS Dolphin ... written by her master George Robertson* (The Hakluyt Society, second series No. XCVIII, 1948) and Charles Darwin, *The Voyage of the Beagle* (Dent, 1959).

Contents

POSTSCRIPT: LANDFALL

Plates:

The Cast

J. Parkinson del.   F. Chambers Sc.

The Cast

Michael Byrne, able seaman & fiddler, two thirds blind.

Ta'oroa, egg, the creator.
Ti'i, boatbuilder, the first man.
Ruata'ata, kindest of fathers, creator of breadfruit tree.
Hiro, handyman of cunning.

Lt. William Bligh, captain *HMS Bounty*.
Fletcher Christian, master's mate, mutineer (d. Pitcairn Island).

George Stewart, midshipman, mutineer (drowned *HMS Pandora*).
'Peggy', his Tahitian wife.

James Morrison, bosun's mate, *Bounty* mutineer (guilty but pardoned). Capt. Edward Edwards (exonerated after wrecking *HMS Pandora*).

Other mutineers mentioned: Charles Churchill, ship's corporal, and Matthew Thompson, able seaman (d. Tahiti); Henry Heildbrandt, Richard Skinner and John Summer, able seamen (drowned *HMS Pandora*); Thomas Burkitt, Thomas Ellison and John Millward, able seamen (hung Spithead); Peter Heywood, midshipman (guilty but pardoned) and William Muspratt, assistant cook (acquitted on technicality); John Mills, gunner's mate, and Isaac Martin and Alexander Smith, alias John Adams, able seamen (d. Pitcairn Island).

Joseph Coleman, armourer, Thomas McIntosh, carpenter's crew and Charles Norman, carpenter's mate (acquitted on Bligh's testimony).

Tavi and Tuiterai, legendary chiefs of Tautira and Papara.
Perfumed Oil, legendary princess.

Pomare, chief of Pare, made King of Tahiti by the mutineers.
Purea, wife of chief of Papara.
Vehiatua, chief of Tautira.

Sun, Moon, Octopus, Shark.

Oro, god of war.
(Douglas L. Oliver (see sources, pp. 890-91) quotes three different traditions for the origins of Oro. I have followed the third).

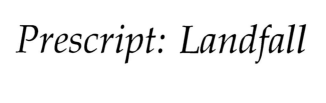

Prescript: Landfall

HMS Dolphin: 1767

June 20: At 9.A.M. we was oblidged to laye too,
espetially as we heard the sea Bracking and making
a great notice on some reefs of Rocks. In a short time
the fogg cleared up, and we now suposed we saw
the long wishd for Southern Continent so often
talkd of, but neaver before seen by any Europeans.
The country had the most beautiful appearance its
posable to Imagin, with great numbers of trees with
flowers of various colours which must certainly bear
some sort of fruit yet unknown to us – but I shall drope
this Discourse as no good spy Glass discovered it to me.

We saw upwards of a hundred canoes betwixt
us and the brakers all padling off towards the ship.
When they came within pistol shot they lookt at our ship
with great astonishment, and padled round and made
signs of friendship to us, holding up Branches of Plantain,
and uttering a long speech of near fifteen minutes.
Some of the sailors Grunted and Cryd lyke a Hogg
then pointed to the shore – oythers crowd Lyke cocks
to make them understand that we wanted fowls.
This the natives of the country understood and Grunted
and Crowd the same as our people, and pointd to the shore
and they brought a good many fine young Girls down
of different colours, some was a light coper collour oyrs
a mullato and some almost if not altogeather White –
This new sight Atract our mens fance a good dale,
and the natives observed it, and made the Young Girls

play a great many droll wanting tricks, and the men
made signs of friendship to entice our people ashoar.
All the sailors swore they neaver saw handsomer made
women in their lives, and declard they would all to a man,
live on two thirds allowance, rather nor lose so fine
an opportunity of geting a girl apiece – even the sick
which hade been on the Doctors list now declard
a Young Girl would make an Excelent nurse and they
were Certain of recovering faster under a Young Girl's
care nor all the Doctor would do for them.

　　　　　　　　All this time
the Bay was lined round with men, women and children,
to see the Onset which was near at hand. But they
still behaved freindly untill a large double canoe
came off from the shore, with several of the Principle
Inhabitance in her. This canoe was observed to hoist some
signall and the very instant all trade broke up, and in a few
secants of time our Decks was full of Great and small
stones, and several of our men cut and Bruisd. This
was so sudden and unexpected that we was some time
before we could find out the caus. We then found
Lenity would not do, therefor applyed to the Great Guns
and gave them a few round and Grape shot which struck
such terrors amongs the poor unhapy wretches that
it would require the pen of Milton's self to describe.

After all this orders was given that the Boats set out,
and in a few minutes Landed and formd on the Beach,
and with hoisting a Pennant took possession of the Island
In His Maj name, and Honourd it with the name
of our Most Gracious sovereign King George the third.

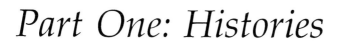

Part One: Histories

Sitodium altile.

Otaheite

Sydney Parkinson pinxit 1769.

I *The Hearing*

The case is Christian's mutiny. But your court
Won't stomach that Christian. It smells of
Mercy. This tale's awash like the *Bounty's*
Bilge with meanings no one wants. Ay, it was
Christian's mutiny. We were all there, you
All saw, Adams, black Matthew, gunner Mills,
By Christ, Adam's mutiny! Jack Adams, John Doe,
Every-man-Jack's mutiny! But your Lords
Need a hanging, not this tale rippling
Irishly like a stone in a green lagoon.

I remember the white untidy beach, my head
A washed up coconut jumping with sandflies.
If my fiddle were jailed and not fathom
Five in the Barrier Reef singing to catfish,
I'd strike up a jig the court martial
Would dance to! Michael Byrne, Irish fiddler,
Two thirds blind, on trial for my life.

> *I kissed that maid and went away,*
> *Says she, Young man, why don't ye stay*

George Stewart, midshipman. That's a truly
Life matter! Gentle George, drowned in leg-irons
In a panic of keys while your Captain Edwards
Jumps ship as light and easy as he's danced
From your court. Tacks his ship on the coral?
Huzzah! Drowns his shipmates? Well away!
And George's bounty, sweet brown Peggy, who
Ever chose a better wife in the South Seas
Or England? Crouched on the poop by the cage
Keening and I could smell the blood, George
Heaving at his chains yelling she was bloodying
The baby and us cursing double Edwards
She was after carving open her scalp
With a shark's tooth.

>*All dark his hair, all dim his eye,*
>*I knew that he had said goodbye.*
>*I'll cut my breasts until they bleed.*
>*His form had gone in the green weed.*

Did she see her midshipman
Dead in Edward's box on Great Barrier Reef?
A life matter truly! And now I recall
The oath he swore her in Matavai bay
He'd never again set foot in muddy
England with its watery sun and broomsticks.
That sweet sundown with the wind offshore

Drunk with blossoms no white man had named,
He held up his left arm to my better eye
And I squinted at a heart with a dart
Through it and a black star. "What's this?"
I warbles, and he says "tattoo." Took him
All day and hurt like blazes. But permanent.
One of their words, tattoo. Strange how we
Needed their lingo to make a landfall.

> *English boy, please tell to me*
> *What is the custom in your country?*

The new Cythera. Two volcanic breasts
And a fern-lined valley. Half a degree
Leeward, you'd miss it. I'll say this for Bligh,
In the whole South Seas he'd smell out one
Breadfruit tree on a rock. But Tahiti
Scuttled us. There were oceans we couldn't
Sail and that island named them: taboo.
Another locution we harboured. We're
All marked with Tahiti, hearts and stars
And commemorations. You, Millward, is it
God's truth you've Tahiti's chart on your yard
And testicles? Morrison, scratching your
Journal of excuses, is your loving groin
Gartered with *Honi soit qui mal y pense?*
How d'you hope to escape hanging after

Pledges like that? Leave Bligh out of it,
Truly the only blind man in Tahiti,
A poor fool with his rules and longitudes
While Michael Byrne, fiddler, kept watch.
Taboo: Christian's mutiny. Ten of us
Of twenty-five still waiting to be hung.

> *King Louis had a prison,*
> *He called it his Bastille,*
> *One day the people tore it down*
> *And made King Louis kneel.*

II *The First Man*

Tahitohito,
> the fifth Age when
> cunning gave birth to mockery.

> First
Was Ta'oroa the egg, tired of loneliness,
> and his wife Stratum Rock,

Ta'oroa of sure bidding, of the cloudless sky,
        who stood over the passage of the reefs.
Ta'oroa was a god's house, his backbone
        the ridgepole, his ribs the buttresses.
Ta'oroa married his daughter Moon
        and moulted red feathers from which grew
        all plants except breadfruit tree.
Ta'oroa conjured Shark God and Rooster
        and Octopus who clasped
        earth to sky, smothering all light until
Ti'i stood forth, the first man,
        and was angry,
Ti'i the boat-builder, clothed in sand,
        was angry demanding
Light and he wrestled with Octopus' eight forearms
        till sky floated free
        shining with starlight and sunlight.
Then Ti'i the fire-maker, the axe-sharpener, was hungry
        and his oven was sealed at daybreak
        and opened at nightfall
        but the meat was raw because
Sun was made drunk by space and hurtled like a meteor
        until Maui his firstborn
Roped his ten rays with ten anchor cables
        and day became a task's length
        and order was complete.

III *The Ship*

Bounty, a word to sail in. We shipped it
South on a year's passage. Nine thousand
Leagues, Bligh boasted, and I believe him.
For facts and cutlass words you'd trust Bligh.
But *Bounty* took his measure. God's humanity
In our navigation, our miraculous draught
Of dolphins. In the larks which sang landfall.
In the albatrosses Bligh stuffed with corn
And cooked like geese. That's *Bounty* reckoning
Bligh, God's munificence turned plunder. What
Was our trade but packeting God's breadfruit
To the slavers? Bounty on a poacher's pelt
Or nigger's poll, or prize ship? Bounty
In the king's shilling? Bounty-jumpers, Bligh
Christened us, bountiful in his contempt.

> *Bounty was a grocer ship,*
> *Pump ship, packet ship,*
> *Sailing on a cruising trip*
> *In the South Pacific.*

So we shipped them a word to brawl over
While they screwed us raw for six-inch nails
They prised below deck from *Bounty's* timbers.

Michael Byrne's *Bounty*? What's a sea trip
To a sightless man? The worst of my voyage
Was Spithead, our salt baptism two mornings
Afore Christ's birth. Such bullying winds
Ambushed us as I never thought to be
Pummelled by. Three nights of it, boats stove
In, cabins awash, beer casks overboard
For all we loitered like a Lime Street whore
With barely a stitch of canvass.

> *The Ol' Man shouts, the pumps stand by,*
> *Oh, we can niver suck her dry,*
> *It's pump or drown the Ol' Man said*
> *Or else damn soon ye'll all be dead.*

Cape Horn
Likewise, the gales like a brick wall and seas
So criss-cross and contrariwise *Bounty*
Jumps backwards like a march hare.

> *O round Cape Stiff in the month of May,*
> *O round Cape Stiff is a bloody long way.*

For the rest
It was pay for a fiddler, and speaking
The truth as an Irishman I liked my perch
On the capstan sawing away, my rib cage
Emptied of the ship's stink, sailing where reels
And hornpipes took me. On a blind voyage
You're corked in, like a ship in a green bottle.
I smuggled from the South Seas two score
Ballads. Now my salt fiddle strikes 'em up
For George's bones jig-jigging in the coral.

iv *The Kindest of Fathers*

The second Age was of trouble when nobles settled
    the high headlands
    and the gentry the quiet bays
And the commoners encroached everywhere, breaking
    down the bamboo fences of the great.
Then there came famine, so cloudless even the chiefs
    ate land crabs and red clay,
But Ruata'ata, kindest of fathers, led his wife and children
    to the mountains to gather ferns
And taking pity, his toes rooted and his fingers branched

and he became Breadfruit tree
Heavy with ripeness and his family feasted, and so trouble
gave birth to wisdom.

v *The Ballad*

Cape of Good Hope. Those old Portuguese
Shipped their lingo with 'em, blessing the storms
With bread and wine. But a blind man harkens.
That Cape had its own rhythms. There's a point
We walked to, George Stewart and me, where oceans
Touch. I never, not even in Ratcliffe Highway,
Heard so many jawbreakers, Hollands, Malay,
Hindustani, a queer breed of nigger English.
Words club you in that town like the smell
Of sweet natches and roast corn after quarters.

Africa's where I twigged Mr Christian.
It turned his head stomping feet on red soil
After the catwalk *Bounty*. He'd been chasing
Butterflies under Table Mountain and caught
A ballad of a white woman and a babe
At a kraal, thirty days hence by the coastline.

That, and her song. She was always after
Hugging the child. There wasn't a man-Jack
Not pierced by this. What women d'you see as I
Tell you, Morrison?

> *Oh lady, have you a daughter fine*
> *Fit for a sailor that's crossed the line?*

A song like that you
Make up your own girl. Christian's was a child,
Northcountry like himself, widow of the wreck
Of an Indiaman. Pale cheeks, hair like tar.
That woman drowned all ours. If Bligh hadn't
Cracked our heads where mightn't we yet be grounded
With gentleman Christian? He'd words. That's
Precipitous in a man that's done no living.

VI *The Third Age*

Now hear of Helen the budding flower, her long hair
      sleek with sandalwood,
Who so bewitched Tuiterai
      the womaniser, chief of Papara,

He sent shafts of feathers to her husband Tavi,
        chief of Tautira,
Begging to possess her for seven days. "Seven nights
        only," he gave his oath,
And would return her in his war canoe with a gift
        of seven fat hogs.
Tavi for all his wife's love was roped by courtesies
        to a fellow chief,
So Helen spent seven nights with Tuiterai the womaniser
        and seven noons in his hut,
And he took the praise name Tuiterai Twin Breasts
        so his courtiers sniggered.
But at the cold star of the eighth cockcrow
        Twin Breasts sang

Why should I give up my treasure,
I, Tuiterai of the six skies?
Tie up the heavens like a net,
Wrestle the clouds of Papara,
Open the net and hang up to dry
The thousand knots that bind us.

Tavi heated his war drums and summoned his canoes
        and laid Papara waste
Carrying Helen home with necklaces of sharks' teeth on
        each of the seven hogs,
While his warriors chased Tuiterai to the cloudbase,

snaring him in a net, and were
Wrestling him to the clifftop to hang up to dry
        when Twin Breasts shouted
"No commoners may execute
        a chief of the fortieth generation."
Tavi's warriors were silenced. Only Tavi
        could kill Tuiterai.
Six days they carried him blindfold along the beaches
        waiting for the warm tides,
And at each cold stream Twin Breasts dipped his hand
        for he knew the touch of the waters.
The seventh cockcrow they brought him to Tavi's house
        and Tavi despaired.
Between vengeance and courtesy was no calm passage.
        Tuiterai Twin Breasts
Was his guest, securer than any elsewhere, and king
        of his house and Helen.

> *Take my wife, Twin Breasts,*
> *You have trapped her in your seine.*
> *I would die for her cloudless beauty,*
> *She is my morning and evening star.*
> *But take my dear wife, Tuiterai,*
> *My heart strings are undone.*

VII *South*

The Pacific, wept by God in his blindness.
You'd steer twelve months on a half-wrong tack
And never hear breakers, the sun dangling so
High above the main mast even I squinted.
In the end the look-out was singing Ahoy
When birds appeared, petrels and albatrosses.
They'd a trick of calling up a south wind
And at cockcrow we were among islands.

> *On the Bounty were the rules*
> *Pump ship, packet ship,*
> *Not for soft and silly fools*
> *In the South Pacific.*

This wasn't discovery. Cook knew 'em already
And that Frenchie they call Buggerville. From
Deptford Dock to the Spithead cathouses
We'd all whistled for the brown girls so
Wet for sailors they'd do it on the beach
With their uncles watching. What we disputed,
Tom Birkett and me eight bells to four
By the lagoon where we supped on green mussels
And Muspratt swore the devil he was poisoned,

Was AD 1773 carved on a trunk. A footprint
Like Defoe's island. Where was that and whose
Knifework was it? Our first landfall we were
Tracking ourselves, imagining shipwreck.

> *Never was there heard a word,*
> *Pump ship, packet ship,*
> *Of the crew that stayed on board*
> *In the South Pacific.*

VIII *The Handyman of Cunning*

So wisdom was made foolish and Hiro flourished,
      handyman of cunning,
Who sat astride the ridgepole of his grandfather's
      school learning
Catches and chants and all poetry's riddles
      before walking.
What is a man's purpose? To build a house
      and get married.
What must I do with a wife? Feed her
      and give her your cherishing.
That would be wasteful. Tell me what

else men do?
Lying, thieving, killing. Good.
        Dishonesty
Is profitable. It will be satisfying to a man.

IX *Breadfruit*

Nippled in your palm and heavy,
Sweating like a green swamp.

    I put my hand upon her thigh,
    Says she, Young man ye're rather high.

X *Tahitohito*

So *Bounty* dropped anchor and we swaggered ashore
        girls draped on our necks
In the fifth age, *tahitohito,* when cunning
        gave birth to mockery.
They twigged at once we were the right gods

for the times.
Our tricks with a foresail made 'em stare
     and our iron was like gold.
But nothing we did showed reverences, and we
     fucked anything that moved.
Then the ballads started. Cook's men were back,
     bleached like lepers,
Stinking like stale milk, our hides tattooed
     with brawling and the cat.
It confirmed the revolution and what better cockshy
     than Bligh himself
With his martinet's livery and his wooden wife
     in *Bounty's* figurehead?
We were *tahitohito,* the fifth age, and their worship
     was disbelief.

Part Two: Shipwreck

Hibiscus. Rosa Sinensis.

otaheite

Sydney Parkinson pinx.[t] 1769

XI *George*

Landfall in Tahiti's hobbling barefoot
Up a steaming path under the plantains,
A girl singing on your arm, steering you
To a ravine with a cliff like Wells Minster,
With ferns cold to the touch, and she says
"That's Tia-auru river", and you remember
The blind current surging from the cave,
Warm with dung, albino with catfish, so high
It took two days climbing into the clouds
And here, you can't believe it, falling as
Rain. Staring up doesn't help. This is rain
And you're homesick but Tia-auru has brimmed
Land's End in the sky and sheered to glass,
Splintering to foam, dropping to nowhere,
A smoking slipstream, tugged by the breezes,
So light in its patter even the cloth-winged
Butterflies flop through its mist, and you
Perch on a flagstone, the girl on your arm,
Her tar hair drenched by this river turned
To summer rain, and you stare at mutiny.

    I'll cut my breasts until they bleed.
    His form had gone in the green weed.

This was George Stewart's chorus. He'd been
Up with Peggy in the mountain summer farm
And the afternoon's descent was like shipwreck.
He gabbled of a pond with floating leaf-palettes
And a girl bathing tits-deep in the lilies.
Ho-hum, I says, where was Peggy? But he
Was beyond gravelling, already marooned
By the green lagoon on the sickle beach,
Bounty's ribs charred on the headland.

    Listening as I was not to your words
    But to the modulations of your voice
    And seeing as you gestured not the glades
    We walked in, only the poised grace
    Of green light on your skin and you pointing,
    I can't now remember what we said
    Or what you showed me, can't begin painting
    Those leaves and vines, that sunlit river bed.

    But since your fingers' pressure on my hand
    That day of mornings, nothing's as it was.
    Nothing seems alien now you understand.
    I deal no more in heartsick ironies.
    This is my home, this still-discovering island,
    Ringed by such shores, such pelican-haunted seas.

                                    So George
In love! Next day they drummed his skin: tattoo!
He held up his left arm to my better eye
And I squints at a heart and a black star.
"What's this?" and he tells me "Tattoo". Took
All day and hurt like blazes. But permanent.

XII *Bligh*

But how would old Bligh consider himself
Politic? Show him seven skies of stars, he'll
Prick 'em. But when he stalked the beaches
In full rig, sweating rank through his spine
And armpits, you'd hear *wei-wei, tahitohito,*
And hoots of belly laughter.

> *Who's the thief?*
> *Tareu the thief*
> *Stole Bligh's anchor-buoy.*

                                    Their women
Got nowhere, not even Queen Purea who knew
She was better bred and made it statecraft

To service her. But this was another
Cook, besotted with his ship. Fingering
Bounty's timbers was stroking his woman.

> *I put my hand upon her hip,*
> *Says she, Young man let's take a trip.*

What crazed 'em were the iron goods and muskets
He showered on mad chief Pomare — so much
It took a mansize sea chest to shut 'em in
With a padlock and clasp, Pomare's people
Not troubling overmuch about ownership.
But Bligh's temper did the rest. When they saw
What tantrums they could wind him to over
Tin pots or a thimble they'd him snared.
Before the end they were pocketing his crew.
They took George Stewart and Churchill, Millward
And Muspratt. They'd ways of thieving the heart
From your breastbone Bligh could never police.

October's moon they made their play. The *Arioi*
Were in town, warrior actors with crimson
Thighs and feather skirts driving the women
Crazy with admiration. The *Arioi* could say
What they like and take what they like and we all
Buzzed how they'd lampoon Bligh. It started
On the *Bounty* with Bligh feeding Pomare

Like a nanny through seven courses of pork.
Upside down, you see, everything reversed.
Then we rowed 'em ashore and hoisted 'em
Under the coconut arches to a clearing
With so many bonfires the *Arioi* called it
Sun-copulating-with-Moon, or the like. Aye, I was
There, with my bum at a fireside and a fistful
Of ribs my fiddle had earned me, marvelling
How on that island I could always make out
Candleflies, like scatters from the sunsets
That had me blinkered. But Bligh was an extra.
They kept him waiting, watching their play.
There were actors who weren't actors, *Arioi*
Who weren't *Arioi* acting, and their argument
Was theft. They sat feasting, keeping Bligh
In audience, till one of 'em would sneak his
Neighbour's pork-knuckle, and they bounced up
And danced in a line:

> *Who's a thief?*
> *Tarue the thief*
> *Stole Bligh's rudder.*

So they'd turned Bligh
Overseer, and perched at their feast again
Till someone colonised a breadfruit slice:

Who's a thief?
Tarue the thief
Stole Bligh's compass.

Then they changed their burlesque, from Bligh
Without bearings to Bligh the woman-hater.
By Christ, I loved it. They're blinder to books
Than Michael Byrne but they read their enemy.
Bligh shouldered the baskets and bolts of calico
And the suckling pig he'd been told to bring 'em
Back and forth from the cutter like poor Jack Tar
To the Big Men staring down from the platform.
There were nine of 'em, lounging on their stools,
Twirling their toes and languid fly-whisks, frowning
Like judges at a fart till one of 'em sang out

I am the comedian of this land
That vibrates with the gun.

He uncurled, all seven foot of him, strutting
Like a bird of paradise and taunted Bligh,
Husband of the *Bounty,* hater of thieves,
Whether he'd children in his own country. So
There was Bligh, untouched by woman, confessing
To fatherhood and, by God, they made him lumber
Back to the cutter for a second forfeit.
This time they'd a speech for him. Pomare

Cued him line by line and he thought 'twas his
Accent convulsed while the *Arioi* sat deadpan:

> *This is the age without meaning,*
> *No payment. just copulation,*
> *Copulation to climax, one after another.*
> *The mouth does not even have to call out,*
> *The eyes say all that is necessary*
> *Until we have made our circle of Tahiti*
> *Copulating, copulating, copulating.*

Bligh stood there cunning in his livery
With the crowd whoop-whooping at every line,
But he couldn't see ourselves in their mirror.
The man thought he was diplomatising, getting
Bounty pregnant with breadfruit on the cheap.

XIII *Christian*

Study, he said, *this land without King George*
To keep raw anger rising in your gorge,
Without a throne, an altar or Bastille
To crush the people with an iron heel,

This soil where natural man's impulses flow
Along the channels mapped by Jacques Rousseau,
Unlike the lands we sailed from with such pains
Where man born free is everywhere in chains.
Who would not chuse to live where Nature proffers
Shelter and dress and food from ample coffers,
Where artificial needs are yet unstudied,
The Horn of Plenty generous and unbloodied.
Who would not chuse to die —

        So the rocking horse
Of his class. It took Christian to mutiny
In couplets. I told him his French hero was
Mad George's pensioner. But Tahiti scarred him
Less than Bligh. Nature. Simplicity. Every
Word he chiselled was heavy with England.
If he'd stayed home he'd have seen his Liberty
And the Bastille burning. Now he's cruising
The South Seas with his skull full of words.

XIV *Possession*

"Boys dream," says our native poet, "of native
Girls bringing breadfruit — whatever they may be."

I put my hand upon her cunt,
Says she, Young man take what ye want.

XV *Mutiny*

Perfumed Oil's hair was a ballad sung
      by the summer wind to a calm ocean
And four brothers harkened and set sail in a canoe
      with four thatched cabins,
But when they anchored off the island
      of Perfumed Oil's inheritance, she was
Away in the woods collecting sweet smelling ferns
      for the arrival she had foretold,
And her servant girl welcomed the brothers, hiding
      the stench of her ordinariness
With scented oils from her mistress's gourds. So three
      brothers were deceived,

Carrying the maid to the canoe where the youngest
      brother kept watch.
Perfumed Oil returned and found her gourds
      and girdle of feathers
Stolen, so she embarked on her surfboard, swimming
      a day and a night
And accosted the eldest brother, "Take me
      up into your vessel",
And the second brother the same and the third
      until the youngest
Took pity, offering her pork ribs and fresh water
      and the safety of his cabin.
But the canoe was becalmed and the air grew foul
      and the servant girl shouted
"See how the impostor has stolen my sweet odour
      and my fresh breeze",
And three brothers were deceived, casting Perfumed Oil
      into the whirlpool
Where Shark God received her in his cavernous mouth
      and sank to his lair.
The sisters in Papeete were preparing for a bride
      but the feather banners
Would not stand upright and the perfume gourds
      cracked, and when
The maid was carried ashore on the tallest man's
      shoulders, she could
Not walk on mats where the sisters set foot freely

but cowered in the latrine.
So the story tumbled out and the youngest brother sailed
       back to the whirlpool,
Pouring oil on the waves and chanting his poems
       till Shark delivered
Shipshape and Bristol fashion the wife
       of his pity and desiring.

Not a strong tale to my Irish mind, needing
Ballast from a tune with a deep undercurrent
Though the stench of my ordinariness maybe
Fogs the finer points. But here's anchorage.
This ballad Christian whistled and begged me
To master and my drowned fiddle humoured him.
For all his mutinies he liked this tale
Of the younger, sea-going brother like himself
Scooping the princess and the inheritance.
I sang it from the capstan not two hours
Afore Bligh's lilibolaro about his missing
Coconuts — aye, the *Arioi* knew about that too.
We were likely Tahitians in winding Bligh
To bedlam over his Christian property.
That night, Christian looked to jump the taffrail
With a surf board and Shark God came for him,
Circling the *Bounty* with one fin showing,
Signalling love from the moon's track in the water.
That's the tale the *Arioi* wove in their dancing,

Christian called back to his island by the god.
But he disobeyed and took the *Bounty* instead
So we're all to stretch necks, the gods not
Winnowing impulses like your English court.

Christian had no bride, just a Catherine
Or two in Papeete. It was gentle George
And brown Peggy had a tale of their own.
But Shark did come. He fired your mutiny
In a clamour for muskets to take pot shots
At death. What happened next was sorcery,
A pother of fulminations and not a man-Jack
Bruised! I was dangling like a hanged man
In the cutter and heard all your contrariness
And the cowardice of those they're calling heroes.

The *Arioi* followed their sense of what fits.
Three years on you've nothing so well shaped.
I'll stay with Shark God and Christian's princess.
If 'twas danced truly, I'd acquit the man.

XVI *The Question*

What was your *Bounty* cellmates? Not a man
Of you nobly mutinous. Did you collar
Bligh on deck in his nightshirt? Then why
Portsmouth, Tom Birkett? It's no harbour
For that history. And Elly, lad, Tom Ellison,
"I'll be sentry over him", will ye? The last
Of the *Bounty* Bligh saw was your arse aloft
Loosing the top gallant. You're a child, Tom,
No pirate. And you're his twin, Heywood. No
Pleading family here. That cutlass. Why did
Your hand touch it? Did you know that daybreak?
D'you know three summers on? Yet you hallooed
Edwards, come to hang you, like a schoolmate.

> *The fiddler took up his fiddle*
> *And merrily he did play*
> *The Scottish jig and hornpipe,*
> *And then the Irish hey.*

Muspratt likewise. A carcase tanned like yours
Should know its mind. I heard the cat, twelve
Lashes, then two dozen and twenty-four more.
Bligh says you're much marked and he should know.
And you, Millward, who never picked your nose but

Churchill ordered you. Or Morrison scribbling
Your journal of exculpation. Why aren't you
Sailing the South Seas in Christian's *Bounty?*
Coleman might cheat the rope, and McIntosh
And Norman. Bligh promised he'll see you right.
The rest of you'll hang for contrariness.

XVII *Oro*

Even the gods hadn't foreseen this sixth Age
      of Horrors
When breadfruit tree's shadow, shook by Ta'oroa,
      moved across Hina-the-Earthbound
And she grinned up at the shade which instructed her
      "Here are Ta'oroa's genitals,
Stand and examine them and insert them."
      So Oro was born,
      Oro the rabid pig
One jaw pointing to the sky, the other
      to the red earth, gaping
For "man-long bananas" on his altar of skulls,
      Oro the sixth finger,
Bandaged bloodily, on the left hand
      of Tahiti the Fish.

XVIII *The Action*

After your mutiny 'twas a different Island.
It made fresh fools of all of us except
George and sweet Peggy. I danced to Papara,
Crazy about the *Arioi* and women, keeping
Downwind of your battles. Old Purea
Liked my fiddle, and I'd as sound a perch
On a canoe in her courtyard as on *Bounty's*
Capstan. I never knew they'd coined Oro
In our mould. When you'd your way, Morrison,
And made that dunce Pomare king, the eyes
Gouged from the sacrifices plucked even
Mine open. Christian's *noblesse oblige*
Made 'em noble savages. Now they were
Primitives and we'd guns.

> *Mit mein niggerum, buggerum, stinkum,*
> *Mit mein niggerum, buggerum, stinkum,*
> *Vell, ve'll climb upon der steeples*
> *Und ve'll spit down on der peoples.*

You want me to sing
Of your wars, Morrison? I can track you
In my twilight, scratching at your book

Of righteousness. I know what you're thinking
To flatter your Lords with. The poor natives
Needed government, did they? You'd found out
They were tribesmen and tribes are hooligans
In the wise reign of our George? That island
Glowed with its bellbirds and candleflies and the sea
In the casuarinas and the courtyards you'd
Dawdle into and squat on a stump and with
Two bars of "Willow willow" have everyone
Quiet as breathing. For you 'twas for sieges,
Stratagems, night marches and ambuscades,
Your stinking groin gartered with *Honi soit,*
And for what blunt end? To make Pomare
King with his wits as addled as our George's!
That's princely flattery, Morrison. That'll
Buy you reprieve.

> *Tweedle-Dee*
> *And Tweedle-dum,*
> *Bow your head*
> *And raise your bum.*

     So Tahiti's tribes came
Against you like they'd never hated Bligh,
Pitching down mountainsides from the nor'west
And west and all points of the compass south
In a real mutiny, one that knew its business.

Only your guns succoured you while Pomare
Clapped his ears against the bang bang of murder.

Don't boast you'd no hand in it. I heard you
At Papara when Pomare despatched
His coronation standard and people smothered
Their cooking fires and hid in the forest. You
Saw for all its feathers, 'twas the Union Jack
And barked fusillades in King George's honour.
English colours, English powder.

> *Pop-pop went the muskets,*
> *Bang went the gun,*
> *Crash went the cannon*
> *And out went the sun.*

Those last days
On Tahiti, we all traipsed like schoolboys
To the temple Pomare had built for Oro,
The war god your taboos bestowed on him.
All your tribes submitted. Only Vehiatua's
People raised their skirts and bared their arses
At your flag. The rest looked to the mountains
When their children were speared through the right
Ear and dragged behind canoes to Pare
And flung before the new king of Tahiti
Who sat with his mouth open while the priests

Skewered their eyeballs with bamboo splints.
                    Aye, it's true.
Pandora saved you, Morrison. Double Edwards
Of all captains, arrested you in your frenzy.

XIX *Shipwreck*

Night on Great Barrier reef and white seas,
Edwards laying to, panicking at fifty
Fathoms, putting about, grounding broadside,
Eleven hours foundering and every Jack-in-office
Jumps ship while thirty-one able shipmates
Drown. It should have sunk him. Yet he swans
From your English court oblivious of shallows!

> *A bully ship with a bully crew*
> *But the captain's a bastard through and through.*

I remember breakers pitching coconuts like
Cannonfire. Then the scalding beach razored
With coral. Shipwreck for George who willed it
By a pond with blue lilies and afterwards
Peggy ripping open her scalp. Does she

Weep he's betrayed her, gone so long? We beached
In our skins, thumping like catfish, and George
Was drowned, and Hanover Henry with his old
Satire our mad king was his uncle's uncle.
Scarface John was dead and young Dick Skinner.

> 'An if we drown while we are young,
> Better to drown than wait to be hung.

So jail's present tense, a restful anchorage.
There's be no burning Bastilles here, only
A long war with the Irish the likely losers.
Your lords have a style of using islands
As cudgels in a war with yourselves. If 'twas
Freedom you sought, Tom Ellison, Tom Birkett,
You should've drifted with your chance. Somewhere
In the South Seas, Christian and Jack Adams,
Black Matthew and Martin and Gunner Mills
Have burned their *Bounty* and launched their wars.
We homed in irons and found Bligh bobbing
And beribboned after a thousand leagues
Fine seamanship, every man-Jack saved
With the salt water inches from his gunnels!

Strange, I could make out candleflies. Show
Bligh seven skies of stars he'll prick 'em, blind
To the bounty dazzling this sightless man.

xx *Sentence*

We took our quarrels with us
And dark imaginings,
We found a laughing people,
We left behind a king.

> *English boy, please tell to me*
> *What is the custom in your country?*

Michael took up his fiddle
And mournfully did play
The Scottish pibroch
And the Irish well-away.

Where are the men who seized the ship
And sailed into the dawn?
Where are the men who dangled?
They'll hang tomorrow morn.

My love weeps in the South Seas
Dark by a calm lagoon
Where coconut flags are silver
In the torchlight of the moon.

Where are the men who seized the ship
And sailed into the night?
My babe's head is bloodied,
My salt-sea bones are white.

Louis was the King of France
Before the Revolution.
Today they cut his big head off
And spoiled his constitution.

Michael took up his fiddle
And merrily he did play
The Scottish jig and hornpipe
And then the Irish hey.

Sweet George, please tell to me
What is the custom in your country?

Postscript: Landfall

HMS Beagle: 1835

October 20: At first light, Tahiti
was in view. As soon as we anchored
in Matavai Bay, we were ringed by canoes.
This was our Sunday, but the Monday
of Tahiti: if the case had been reversed,
we should not have received a single
visit; for the injunction not to launch
a Sabbath canoe is strictly obeyed.

> *She wears red feathers*
> *And a hoola hoola skirt,*
> *She wears red feathers*
> *And a hoola hoola skirt.*
> *She lives on*
> *Just coconuts*
> *And fish from the sea,*
> *A rose in her hair*
> *A gleam in her eye*
> *And a love in her heart for me.*

Everyone brought conch shells for sale.
Tahitians now understand money and much
prefer it to parrot feathers or nails.
The various coins, however, of English
and Spanish denomination puzzle them;
they never seem to think the small silver
quite secure until changed into dollars.

I work in a London bank
Respectable position.
From nine to three
They serve you tea
But ruin your disposition.
Each night at the music hall
Travelogues I'd see
And once a pearl
Of a native girl
Came smiling right at me.

There are many who scorn the missionaries'
improvements and dub Presbyterian the ban
on night revelry and the nose flute.
Such reasoners never compare the present
island with that of twenty years ago. They
forget, or will not remember, that human
sacrifices, an idolatrous priesthood,
profligacy unparalleled, bloody wars — all
these have been abolished: and dishonesty,
intemperance and licentiousness reduced.

Tired of the London bank
I started out a sailing.
Fourteenth day
From Mandalay
I spied her from the railing.
She knew I was on the way
Waiting, and was true.
She said, you son
Of an Englishman,
I dreamed last night of you.

Queen Pomare was persuaded to dine
on the Beagle. Four boats were sent
and the yards manned on her Majesty's
coming on board. The Tahitians behaved
most properly. They begged for nothing
and seemed content with their presents.
The Queen is a large, graceless woman,
with only one Royal attribute: a perfect
immovability of expression under all
circumstances, and that a rather sullen one.
Rockets were fired. After each explosion
a deep "ah!" echoed from all points
the moonlit bay. Our sailors' shanties were
much admired. Of one, the Queen declared
"It most certainly could not be a hymn".

> *I'm back here in London town*
> *And though it may seem silly,*
> *She's here with me*
> *And you should see*
> *Us stroll down Piccadilly.*
> *The boys at the London bank*
> *I know they hold their breath.*
> *She sits with me*
> *And drinks her tea*
> *Which tickles them to death.*

Unwittingly, I was the means of my companions
breaking their own laws. I had with me
a flask of spirits, which they could not
refuse to partake of: but as often as they
drank they put their fingers before their
mouths, and uttered the word "Missionary".

ROYALTY THEATRE.

WELL-STREET, near GOODMAN'S-FIELDS.

To continue every Evening during the Summer Seafon, with a Variety of ENTERTAINMENTS.

THIS EVENING, May 3, will be prefented
A new Mufical Piece, called

TAR against PERFUME:

Or, The Sailor Preferred.

A new Dance, called

The MERRY BLOCK-MAKERS:

By Monf. Ferrere, Mad. Fuozzi, Mad. Ferrere, Mr. Bourke, &c.

A new Mufical Piece, called

A PILL for the DOCTOR:

Or, The TRIPLE-WEDDING.

A favourite Song by Mifs DANIEL.

The whole to conclude with (never performed) a Fact, told in Action, called

The PIRATES:

Or, The Calamities of Capt. BLIGH.

Exhibiting a full Account of his Voyage, from his taking leave at the Admiralty, and fhewing the Bounty falling down the River Thames—the Captain's reception at Otaheite, and exchanging the Britifh Manufactures for the Bread Fruit—with an Otahcitean Dance—an exact reprefentation of the Seifure of Capt. Bligh, in the Cabin of the Bounty by the Pirates, with the affecting fcene of forcing the Captain and his faithful followers into the Boat—their Diftrefs at Sea, and Repulfe by the Natives of Timur—their miraculous arrival at the Cape of Good Hope, and their friendly reception by the Governor.

Dances and Ceremonies of the Hottentots on their Departure, and their happy arrival in England.

The Doors to be opened at Half paft Five, and to begin at Half paft Six o'Clock precifely.—Boxes, 3s. 6d.—Pit, 2s. 6d.—1ft Gallery, 1s. 6d.—Upper Gallery, 1s.—Places for the Boxes may be taken at the Stage Door of the Theatre, from Ten till Three o'Clock every Day!   Vivant Rex & Regina.

Other books by Landeg White include:

***For Captain Stedman: Poems* (Peterloo Poets, 1983)**

'For what it's worth, halfway through 1984, I rated Landeg White's *For Captain Stedman* the best collection of poetry published in 1983. I'd not come across his poetry before but knew his name as the author of by far the best book yet published on V.S. Naipaul — precise, perceptive, sympathetic and beautifully written. And those are qualities characteristic of his poetry too, put to the service of a highly cultured, artistically disciplined imagination.' — *Poetry Wales*

'White deploys his verse forms — *terza rima,* syllabics, stress-count lines, free verse — with a fine ear for ironic aptness: *For Captain Stedman* is a sensitive, carefully crafted collection, which besides its alert colonial commentaries offers other pleasures — West Indian speech patterns zestfully recreated, or an evocative description of flamingoes — that make highly enjoyable reading.' — *Times Literary Supplement*

***Magomero: Portrait of an African Village* (Cambridge U.P., 1987)**

'Few other books I can think of so effectively capture the authentic flavour of an African community over an extended period of time. Certainly, there is none that does it with such humour and such grace.' — *Journal of African History*

'... a minor masterpiece ... a perfect example of how to explain great issues by looking at their effects on the lives of little people.' — *American Historical Review*

'... a masterpiece of historical writing.' — *Africana Journal*

'... vivid and gripping.' — *New Society*

Landeg White